Favourite sport

Favourite food

Favourite animal

Favourite artist

More favourite things

Brownie
Annual 2006

Brownie fun

Being a Brownie is great fun! Brownies do all sorts of exciting activities as part of their Brownie Adventure.

Safety symbol

On some pages you'll see this symbol, to remind you that you might need a bit of help with the activity. If there isn't a symbol but you're still not sure, ask for help anyway.

Be safe

Badge link

On most pages of this amazing Brownie Annual 2006 there's a badge link. This shows that the ideas and activities on that page link to a Brownie badge. If you want to find out what you need to do to get the badge, look it up in the Brownie Badge Book. Remember, when you do a badge, always do your best.

BADGE LINK

Friend to animals

Stay safe

You should be able to have a go at everything in your Brownie Annual 2006, but sometimes it's wise to ask an adult you know for help. You can still do it yourself, just make sure the adult says it's okay and is watching.

Your special Brownie saying

Lend A Hand

Brownie Promise

I promise that I will do my best:
To love my God,
To serve the Queen and my country,
To help other people
and
To keep the Brownie Guide Law.

Sixer tips

When you see this sign, you will find hints and ideas for things you could do with your Six at Brownie meetings. Why not suggest them to your Brownie Guider or talk about them in Pow-wow?

Brownie Law

A Brownie Guide thinks of others before herself and does a Good Turn every day.

My Brownie web safe code

When using the world wide web, I promise:

★ to agree rules with my parents or guardians about the best way for me to use the computer and the world wide web.

★ not to give out my home address or telephone number without permission.

Web safe

★ not to give out the name or address of my school without permission.

★ not to agree to meet anyone who I contact on the web, unless my parents or guardians say it is all right and go with me.

★ not to put my photograph onto a website.

★ to tell my parents, guardians, teacher or Guider if I find something on the web that worries or upsets me.

With thanks to the Girl Scouts of the USA for the ideas contained within this warning for children.

Contents

The Brownies who appear in this Annual are from the 7th and 8th Upper Tooting Brownie Packs and the 1st Forest Hill Brownie Pack.

Special thanks to: Amanda Bailey at the RSPCA; missdorothy.com Ltd; Kellie Rollings and Rob McNeil at WWF; Victoria Smith at Munro & Forster; Felicity Roocke.

Written by Mariano Kälfors apart from: 5-A-DAY delights, Hair-clipping fun, Seasonal organic treats and Winter Olympic winners by Kate Sheppard; Miss Dorothy by Claire Britcher at missdorothy.com Ltd; Super Brownie goes global by Alison Griffiths. The Polar Bear written by Kate Fenning.

Cover photographs by Laura Ashman.
Brownie photographs by Laura Ashman.

Brownie Annual 2006: an official publication of Girlguiding UK.
© The Guide Association 2005

All Brownie and Guide photographs © The Guide Association.
All other photographs © as aknowledged on appropriate pages.

Published by Girlguiding UK
17–19 Buckingham Palace Road
London SW1W 0PT
Website www.girlguiding.org.uk

Girlguiding UK is an operating name of The Guide Association. Registered charity number 306016. Incorporated by Royal Charter.

Girlguiding UK Trading Service ordering code 6005
ISBN 0 85260 222 7

Readers are reminded that during the lifespan of this publication there may be changes to Girlguiding UK's policy, or legal requirements, that will affect the accuracy of information contained within these pages.

Patron HM The Queen
President HRH The Countess of Wessex
Chief Guide Jenny Leach
Brownie Adviser Sue Waller
Brownie Programme Coordinator Annie Vine
Project Editor Mariano Kälfors
Project Designer Heather Peters
Designer Caroline Keyzor
Cover Design Heather Peters
Production Les Girling
Colour repro InTouch Group plc
Printed by Scotprint

Girlguiding UK

International Children's Games

Have a go at these puzzles inspired by the International Children's Games this year in Bangkok, Thailand.

Spot the difference

Illustrated by Andi Good

How many balls?

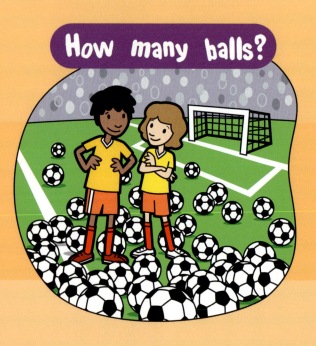

In the water

Which of these two swimmers are exactly alike?

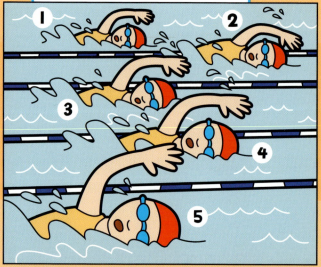

Word maze

Find some of the cities that have already hosted the International Children's Games since 1968.

Coventry

Cleveland

Hamilton

Plock

```
I E P I A T S G Y H
G N J U N A E R A A
R M L N I N T M R G
F H A D E N I T O R
C L E V E L A N D A
A M A V T P E O G Z
N F O O L O M V H U
Q C N O N O R G O L
J S C A N D O R R A
P K H H K H Z B V E
```

Patra

Graz

Medias

Velenje

Taipei

Andorra

Geneva

Logrono

What order?

Lizzie is practising for her table tennis match, but what order should she hit all the balls coming at her?

Find the missing piece

How did you do? Check the answers on page 76!

Winnie Lee

Wildlife in danger

On land or underwater, in jungles or on plains, animals are threatened by human activities.

Giant pandas

Pandas are related to bears. They are vegetarians, spending almost 14 hours a day eating bamboo. Today there are only 1,600 pandas left in the world because their homes, the bamboo forests, are being destroyed for firewood and farming. If pandas were to completely disappear, the world would lose a lovable animal that has managed to survive for 3 million years.

Tigers

The tiger is the largest and most powerful cat in the world. It sits at the very top of the food chain, meaning that it eats other animals but is never eaten itself. A hundred years ago there were as many as 150,000 tigers in Asia. Today there are around 5,100 to 7,500 left. Tigers are disappearing for many reasons. Their natural habitat is vanishing – because of human overcrowding – and with it their prey. Tigers are also hunted illegally.

Rhinos

Rhinos, found in Asia and Africa, are one of the largest land animals in the world. There used to be dozens of different rhino species but only five are left. Rhinos are nature's gardeners, they spread plant seeds when roaming, which helps other wildlife to survive. Rhinos are disappearing because people hunt them for their horns. Many people wrongly believe they have magical powers. Much work is being done to stop the illegal hunting of the rhino.

Whales and dolphins

Whales and dolphins are cetacean mammals. This means that they need to breathe air like us. Cetaceans are good indicators of healthy sealife, if they are healthy then the oceans and other creatures in the ocean are healthy too. Whales and dolphins are in danger from hunting, pollution and – the biggest threat to their survival – fishing nets. Over 300,000 are accidently caught and die in nets each year.

BADGE LINK

Great apes

There are four kinds of great apes: gorillas, chimpanzees and bonobos (found in Africa) and orangutans (found in Asia). Of all animals, great apes most resemble humans – for example, chimpanzees have almost exactly the same genes as us! The most endangered great ape is the mountain gorilla, there are only 700 left! The biggest threats to great apes are hunting and the destruction of their natural habitat.

Marine turtles

Marine turtles have been around for over a hundred million years. This means that they were around with the dinosaurs! There are seven types of marine turtles, six of which are endangered. Marine turtles live in the oceans, but need to come ashore to lay eggs. They are disappearing because of hunting, fishing nets, the destruction of their nesting areas, pollution in the oceans and much more.

WWF®

To find out more about endangered wildlife and how you could help save them, visit the WWF website at www.wwf.org.uk . With your Pack, you could adopt an animal directly or find out how to receive an adoption box.

Web safe

PANDA MOSAIC

Mosaic art was first done by the Ancient Romans, Greeks and Egyptians. Have a go at it with this panda art.

1 Wash the eggshells in warm water then place on newspaper and leave to dry. When dry, paint half the eggshells in white and half in black paint. Leave to dry.

2 Place tracing paper over the panda pattern provided and trace around the outline with a pencil.

Place carbon paper face down on the cardboard and place the tracing on top. Trace over the outline with a pencil then remove tracing paper and carbon paper.

3

Apply PVA glue to one area of the design. Break the eggshells into smaller pieces and press firmly onto the wet glue to break up further.

4

PVA GLUE

Use the toothpick to push the pieces apart to leave small gaps in between.

5

Illustrated by Linzie Hunter

Continue applying glue and black- or white-coloured eggshells to the different parts of the panda until finished. Leave to dry.

6

Renewable energy

A source of energy that does not run out or can be replenished quickly is called renewable energy. Five types of renewable energy used most often are: wind, water, the sun, biomass and geothermal.

Wind

You may have heard of windmills long ago being used to pump water and to mill flour. Today we have windmills that create electricity! These are called wind turbines and can be big enough to power an entire school, or small enough to power a phone box.

Geothermal

The centre of the earth is VERY hot and this is called geothermal energy. In parts of the world, power plants can collect heat from the earth's core, as steam, and use it to turn turbines to create electricity. Water can also be pumped from hot underground lakes to heat homes.

Sun

The sun has been providing us with solar energy for billions of years! Today there is already technology that turns sunlight directly into electricity! This is called photovoltaic energy and it is used in a lot of calculators. Solar energy is also used today to heat water in homes and other buildings that have solar panels.

Water

As well as being lots of fun, water can be used to create power. Today water flowing in rivers is used by machines called hydro turbines to make electricity. People are also trying to develop similar machines that can use the power of waves and tides.

Biomass

Biomass refers to plants and trees that have stored energy from the sun, and which is released through burning. Today's farmers grow specific crops as biomass fuel, like straw, sugar cane and poplar trees. Even rubbish and animal droppings can be used to provide heating and create electricity!

Make a turbine

Want to know how a turbine works? Try this simple experiment.

You need

- a clean empty 1 litre juice carton with a screw top lid • string • a sharpened pencil • some water in a jug • masking tape

1 With the pencil, punch a hole on the bottom right hand corner of each side of the carton.

Be safe

2 Make another hole at the top, push the string through and tie securely.

3 Tape up each hole.

4 Hang the carton freely from a low tree branch where it doesn't matter if the ground gets wet. Fill it with water.

5 Pull off the tape on one corner and watch what happens. Pull the rest of the tape off corner by corner and watch.

You'll see that the water pours out of the small hole and its force causes the carton to turn; the more holes there are, the faster it turns.

This is how a turbine works, some using water, some steam, some wind, but all connected to a generator that makes electricity when it is turned.

Illustrated by Rosie Benham

Renewable

Reduce, reuse or recycle?

How many things in this kitchen can we recycle, reuse or use less of (reduce)?

Illustrated by Nick Diggory

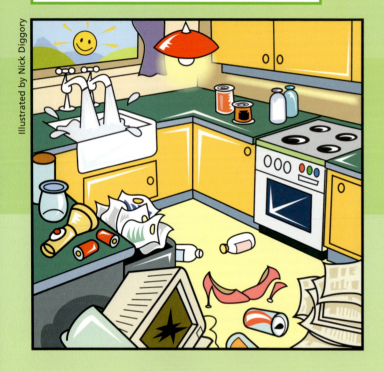

How many?

How many wind turbines can you spot on this wind farm?

Complete the jigsaw

Find the missing jigsaw piece for this solar-panelled house.

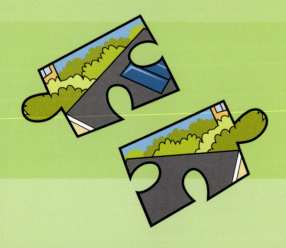

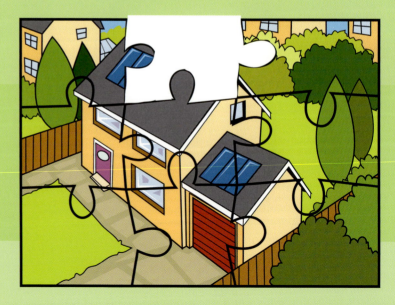

riddles

Renewable energy spots

Circle 6 things that can be used as energy resources.

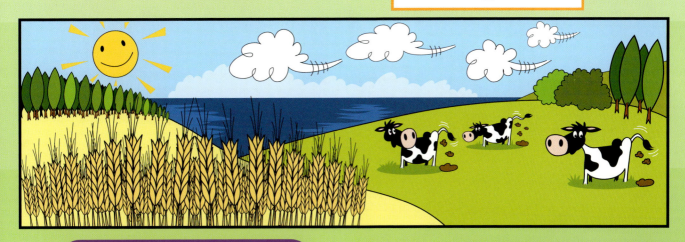

Spot ten differences

How did you do? Check the answers on page 76!

One old Oxford ox

Illustrated by Claire Chrystall

One old Oxford ox opening oysters;
Two teetotums totally tired trying to trot to Tadbury;
Three tall tigers tippling tuppenny tea;
Four fine foxes fanning fainting friars;
Five flighty flibbertygibbets foolishly fishing for flies;
Six sportsmen shooting snipes;
Seven Severn salmon swallowing shrimps;
Eight Englishmen eagerly examining Europe;
Nine nimble noblemen nibbling noodles;
Ten tinkers tinkling upon ten tinder-boxes with ten tenpenny tacks;
Eleven elephants elegantly equip'd;
Twelve talkative tailors trimming tartan trousers.

Anon

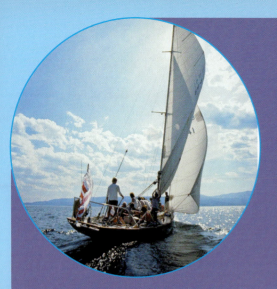

Sail away

What do you know about sailing and boats? Investigate this amazing activity.

How it all began

Humans have been sailing for thousands of years. Once upon a time it was the only way to travel across great distances of water. Sailing is mainly a sport today, and is about enjoying two natural elements – wind and water – and learning to control them.

Sailing boats

Boats come in many shapes and sizes, but all have five things in common. All sailing boats have a hull, which is the floating body of the boat. They have a mast, which is the pole that supports the sails, and of course, they have sails – big pieces of fabric that catch the wind and therefore moves the boat. Sailing boats also have lots of ropes used to tie down and control the sails. Lastly they have underwater fins – one to steer with, called the rudder, and one to balance and keep the boat upright.

More about hulls

Sailing boats can have more than one hull. A monohull has one hull, these are called either dinghies or keelboats (also called yachts) depending on their size. A multi-hull sailing boat has more than two hulls. A two-hulled boat is called a catamaran, one with three is called a trimaran and giant multihulls exist that have four or more hulls.

Masts and sails

Sailing boats can have more than one mast and, likewise, more than one sail. The more sails, the more wind the boat will catch and the faster and farther it can go. The two types of sails are the mainsail attached to the mast and the smaller jib furthest up front.

BADGE LINK

Watersports

Tacking and gybing

The two essential sailing manouevres are called tacking and gybing. These are used to change the direction of the boat. Tacking turns the front end of the boat, the bow, while gybing turns the back end, the stern.

Sailing heroines

One of the most famous sailors in the world today is our own Ellen MacArthur. She started sailing as a little girl and went on to break the world record for being the fastest to sail on her own around the world non-stop. Another famous sailor is Shirley Robertson, who has won two olympic gold medals over two olympic games.

How do I do that?

There are many ways to learn to sail. Most young people learn on small dinghies that are easy to manage. Owning a dinghy isn't something we can all do though, so another way to learn is to join a sailing club. As an adult, you could also learn to sail by becoming a crew member on a big yacht.

If you want to find out more about sailing or even how you could take it up visit **www.rya.org.uk** and **www.gbrsailing.org.uk** . Always remember to follow your web safe code when using the web.

Web safe

SEASHELL BEACH HAT

Create the perfect beach wear for the summer!

You need

a plain straw or fabric beach hat ★ shells, especially fan-shaped, of all sizes ★ fabric glue (you can also use a hot glue gun but only with an adult supervising) ★ natural dye ingredients if using (see Shell dyes box)

1 Wash the shells if newly collected from the beach and leave to dry. If you like, dye the shells overnight for lots of groovy colours. Look at the natural dye suggestions for how.

2 Rinse the shells the next day and allow to dry. On a work surface, arrange the shells in several different patterns that you like. Try arranging in various flower patterns, as butterflies and so on.

Illustrated by Stuart Lynch

Shell dyes

Lavender
Soak the shells overnight in grape juice.

Red
Save the skins from red onions and boil with the shells for 30 minutes to an hour. Leave to soak overnight. The more skins you use the darker the red will be.

Yellow
Add a teaspoon of tumeric and half a teaspoon vinegar to a cup of hot water and leave shells to soak overnight.

Pink

Soak the shells in cranberry juice or juice from pickled beetroot overnight.

Brown
Add a tablespoon of instant coffee and half a teaspoon of vinegar to a cup of hot water and leave shells to soak overnight.

Violet
Add violet blossoms to hot water and leave shells to soak overnight.

Green
Add a quarter teaspoon of bicarbonate of soda to a bowl of violet water (see above) and leave shells to soak overnight.

3 Stuff the hat with paper towels or crumpled newspaper to create a solid surface for gluing. Using plenty of fabric glue, start gluing the shells onto the hat according to your pattern designs. You will need to be patient, as the gluing process can take a while. Leave the hat to dry completely.

Illustrated by Liz McIntosh

My year 2006

Keep track of all the exciting days you are looking forward to this year!

January

1	January **New Year's Day**
26	January **Australia Day**
29	January **Chinese New Year**
31	January **Hijra**

My special dates

○ January ⬭
○ January ⬭

April

13	April **Passover begins**
16	April **Easter Sunday**
23	April **St George's Day**

My special dates

○ April ⬭
○ April ⬭

February

10	February **Winter Olympics begin (Turin, Italy)**
14	February **Valentine's Day**
22	February **World Thinking Day**
28	February **Shrove Tuesday**

My special dates

○ February ⬭
○ February ⬭

May

1	May **May Day Bank Holiday**
8	May **World Red Cross Day**
13	May **Buddha Day**
25	May **Ascension Day**

My special dates

○ May ⬭
○ May ⬭

March

1	March **St David's Day**
15	March **Commonwealth Games begin (Melbourne, Australia)**
17	March **St Patrick's Day**
26	March **Mothering Sunday**

My special dates

○ March ⬭
○ March ⬭

June

9	June **FIFA World Cup begins (Germany)**
11	June **Whit Sunday**
15	June **Father's Day**
21	June **Longest Day**

My special dates

○ June ⬭
○ June ⬭

Illustrated by Michaela Blunden

July

1   July **Canada Day**
4   July **Independence Day (USA)**
14   July **Bastille Day (France)**

My special dates

◯ July _____

◯ July _____

October

1   October **Yom Kippur**
21   October **Diwali**
24   October **Eid al Fitr**
31   October **Hallowe'en**

My special dates

◯ October _____

◯ October _____

August

25   August **Summer Bank Holiday**
     (except Scotland)

My special dates

◯ August _____

◯ August _____

November

5   November **Bonfire Night**
20   November **Universal Children's Day**
30   November **St Andrew's Day**

My special dates

◯ November _____

◯ November _____

September

17   September **International Day of Peace**
22   September **Rosh Hashanah**
24   September **Ramadan begins**
27   September **Grandparents' Day**

My special dates

◯ September _____

◯ September _____

December

16 December **Hanukkah**
21 December **Longest night**
25 December **Christmas Day**
31 December **New Year's Eve**

My special dates

◯ December _____

◯ December _____

What is organic food?

Have you ever heard of food being described as 'organic'? Do you know what it means? Test your knowledge with this fun quiz!

1. What does 'organic' mean?
a) It's an organ-grinding monkey.
b) It can refer to a healthy and sustainable way of growing food.
c) It's a very nice smelling herb used in cooking.

3. How does growing organic food help the environment?
a) Producing food organically helps to improve the health of the soil, so it can stay fertile and keep providing nutrients.
b) Organic food isn't produced using methods or chemicals that harm the environment, humans or animals.
c) Both of the above.

2. How is organic farming different from normal farming?
a) Normal farming uses tractors, organic farming uses horses.
b) Organic farmers work only at night, other farmers in daytime.
c) Organic farming uses ways to grow food that are better for the environment.

4. Is organic food only what grows out of the ground?
a) No. Livestock can also be farmed in an organic way that's better for everyone including the animals themselves.
b) No. Anything farmed on the moon also counts.
c) Yes.

BADGE LINK

Environment

5. How can I tell if something in a supermarket is organic?
a) It will normally tell you on the food packaging if it is.
b) Don't worry, it's really obvious.
c) You can't find organic food in supermarkets, you need to pick it from the ground yourself.

6. Where is organic food grown?
a) Everywhere! But the closer it is grown to you the better it is for the environment because it doesn't have to travel very far in lorries and planes to get to the shops, which creates less pollution.
b) Buckingham Palace.
c) In great big barrels.

7. Can anyone grow organic food?
a) No. You have to learn from a very wise owl in Brownieland.
b) Only if they've been chosen by the organic fairy.
c) Yes! If you like getting mucky, have a garden or an allotment, you could do it too!

Want to find out more about organic food? Visit **www.hdra.org.uk** and **www.organicgarden.org.uk** . Always remember to follow your web safe code when visiting any website.

Web safe

Get them all right? Check on page 77!

SEASONAL ORGANIC

Use organic ingredients where possible in these seasonal dishes.

SPRING SPECIAL – SCRAMBLED EGGS

Celebrate Easter and the coming of spring with our egg-tastic recipe. This recipe serves two people.

You need

4 eggs ★ 15g butter ★ salt and pepper ★ 50g Cheddar, grated

1. Beat the eggs in a bowl with a pinch of salt and pepper.

2. Melt the butter in a wide frying pan over a medium heat. Pour in the eggs and stir constantly with a wooden spoon. While there's still some liquid egg left, add the cheese. Keep stirring until all the liquid has just gone.

3. Serve immediately with toast or on a toasted bagel.

SUMMER – GUACAMOLE

You need

2 large, ripe avocados ★ 2 large ripe red tomatoes, peeled, deseeded and finely chopped ★ juice and zest of 1 unwaxed lime ★ 15g fresh coriander, finely chopped ★ salt and pepper to season

Be safe

1. Cut the avocado in half and remove the stone. Peel the fruit – this can get messy!

2. Either place all the ingredients in a blender or food processor and mix until smooth or put in a bowl and mash together with a fork.

3. Serve as a dip with crisps, breadsticks or vegetables, such as carrots and celery, chopped into sticks.

Illustrated by Claire Chrystall

TREATS

AUTUMN – FRUITY MUFFINS

You need

350g plain flour ★ 1 tbs baking powder ★ 1½ tsp ground cinnamon ★ 75g butter, melted ★ 2 eggs, beaten ★ 275ml milk ★ 75g caster sugar ★ 1 apple, peeled, cored and finely chopped ★ 2 plums, stoned and finely chopped ★ 12 muffin paper cases ★ 12–hole muffin tin

BADGE LINK

Cook

Cook

1 Sieve the flour, baking powder and cinnamon into a large bowl.

2 Add the butter, eggs and milk and stir together. Stir in the sugar, plums and apple.

Milk

Sugar

3 Stand the muffin cases in the muffin tin and fill them two-thirds full with the mixture. Bake for 25 minutes at 200°C/Gas Mark 6.

WINTER – CHOCOLATE AND ORANGE TART

You need

350g plain fairtrade chocolate, broken into pieces ★ 300ml double cream ★ 90g butter ★ juice of 1 orange ★ 18 ready-made mini tartlet pastry shells

1 Melt the chocolate, cream and butter together in a heatproof bowl over a saucepan of barely simmering water. Be careful not to let the bowl touch the water.

2 Remove the bowl from the heat and stir in the orange juice. Cover the mixture with clingfilm and refrigerate until cold.

3 Spoon the filling into the tartlet shells or pipe it in using an icing bag.

I want to be...

What would you like to do when you grow up? Maybe one of these?

A vet!

Treating furry patients,
weighing pets,
clipping claws,
giving shots,
making animals feel better!

A policewoman!

Wearing uniform,
keeping order,
protecting others,
solving crimes,
catching crooks!

A scientist!

Splitting atoms,
observing cells,
studying fossils,
predicting weather,
discovering vaccines!

Illustrated by Martina Farrow

A doctor!

Listening to hearbeats,
taking pulses,
checking temperatures,
giving medicine,
treating unwell people!

An architect!

Drawing,
designing,
planning and
building homes,
airports, shopping malls!

A fashion designer!

Designing clothes,
choosing colours,
picking fabrics,
setting trends,
attending fashion shows!

Year of the dog puzzlers

Have a go at these teasers inspired by Chinese astrology

Animal scramble

Unscramble the letters to name the 12 different animals represented in the Chinese horoscope.

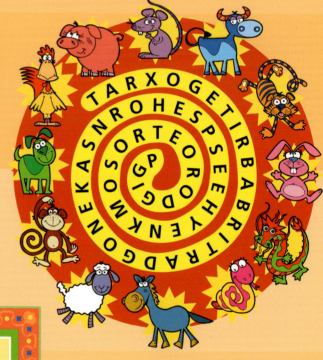

Buddha's maze

According to legend, the 12 animals of the Chinese horoscope were chosen by the Buddha himself. Can you help all 12 of them find their way through the mazy forest to him? Which animal will get there first?

Illustrated by John Hallett

Missing piece

Find the correct missing piece to complete the jigsaw.

Word maze

Find the words linked to the 12 animals in Chinese astrology.

BARK   HISS   ROAR
CHEESE   LETTUCE   SNORT
CROW   MOO   TREES
FIRE   NEIGH   WOOL

N	C	Q	G	V	S	L	F	T	R
C	H	E	E	S	E	N	U	B	O
S	V	X	W	N	E	T	O	N	A
S	T	T	E	C	C	T	W	R	R
I	H	I	R	Q	U	E	O	Y	T
H	G	O	U	T	T	R	O	B	B
H	W	O	R	C	T	I	L	L	Y
F	N	E	O	Y	E	F	M	Q	J
G	E	D	Z	M	L	B	A	R	K
S	M	M	Z	E	C	N	O	O	U

Monkey tricks

Monkey has played a trick on dog and hidden his favourite bone. Can you follow the correct thread to find it?

How did you do? Check the answers on page 77!

Brownie Annual 2006   37

Use your hands not your feet!

The basketball dribble

Basketball originated in America over 100 years ago. Bouncing a ball one-handed is one of the key skills to playing basketball. You can learn this skill on your own with a decent sized rubber ball that bounces.

When dribbling, use the tips of your fingers to push the ball. Never slap the ball and keep your dribbling hand always on top of the ball. All the movement should come from your wrist and forearm.

Don't bounce the ball too high or too low, keep it between knee and waist height. Only one hand at a time can bounce the ball.

Photographs by Laura Ashman

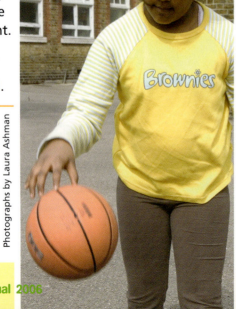

Practise dribbling from a stationary position until you have the basic technique, then try moving around. Practise until you can dribble:

- without looking at the ball
- equally well with both hands.

The volleyball pass

Volleyball, like basketball, is over 100 years old. The pass is one of the key skills in volleyball. You'll need a friend to practise this with, and the ball shouldn't be too hard.

When receiving a pass, have your legs shoulder width apart – one slightly in front of the other – knees slightly bent. Join your hands together with the thumbs parallel to each other. Extend your arms out from your body, parallel to your thighs.

Have your friend throw the ball gently towards you. Make contact with the ball just above the wrists, extend your legs slightly, moving the arms slightly forward and upward. Your legs should propel the ball back to your friend, not your arms.

Take turns practising this skill until:

🏀 you can 'pass' the ball straight back to your friend eight times in a row

🏀 you and your friend can 'pass' the ball back and forth to each other six times in a row.

The netball chest pass

Over one million girls and women play netball regularly. The chest pass is the most commonly used pass in netball. Practise with a friend.

Hold the ball properly by forming a W with your hands behind the ball so your thumbs are together in the centre and your fingers spread out.

Step forward with one foot as you push through with the ball. Keep your elbows close to your body when pushing through.

As you release the ball, straighten your arms and fingers to transfer as much energy as possible to the ball. Look at the person you are passing to, not the ball.

Practise this skill with your friend, increasing the distance between you as your passing improves.

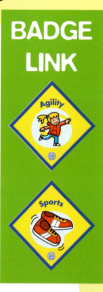

Brownie pen pals!

Want a Brownie penfriend from another country?

Write to me!

A pen pal is a different sort of friend. A penfriend is someone from far away you can become buddies with by exchanging letters, postcards, emails and photos. This form of friendship has been around for a very long time, probably for as long as people have been writing to each other.

Be a pal

A lot of children from non-English speaking countries love to have penfriends from the UK because it helps them to learn and improve their English. Likewise, if you are learning another language at school, a pen pal to practise with could be very helpful.

You've got mail!

Getting a letter through your letterbox with your name on it and a stamp from another country is the most exciting thing about having a Brownie pen pal. You never know what you will find in the envelope and what amazing facts your penfriend will tell you about herself, her unit and where she lives. In turn, she will be very curious to find out all about you and your world!

Find a global buddy

Some of the countries where you can make Brownie friends include Australia, Austria, Belgium, Czech Republic, Denmark, Finland, France, Germany, Greece, Hong Kong, Ireland, Scotland, Norway, Singapore, Slovakia, South Africa, Sweden, Israel, Kenya, New Zealand, Taiwan, Uganda and Wales. Can you find all these countries on the world map?

BADGE LINK

Writer

World cultures

World guiding

Cool Nordics

Brownies from the nordic countries Sweden, Denmark, Finland and Norway are particularly keen to make Brownie friends in the UK. People from nordic countries often love to travel and can speak many languages. What a cool friend that would be!

WAGGGS

Brownies from Hong Kong

Friend for life

Penfriends often continue writing to each other for years and years, eventually visiting each other when they're older and becoming lifelong friends. Imagine how exciting it would be to travel and meet a pen pal for the first time!

Sixer tip

With your Six, why not write a letter to a group in another country about your Brownie Adventure? Ask your Leader for help.

How?

There are two ways to find an overseas Brownie pen pal. With your Leader's help you could contact pen pals at CHQ or visit the website www.girlguiding.org.uk/international to find out about how to apply for one. Another way is to create a Unit Link with a unit in a different country. American Brownies for example love to link with British ones! Your Guider would need to apply on your unit's behalf.

Web safe

The Polar Bear

'It was seven foot tall and covered in bright white fur.' Isobel read aloud to her Brownie Pack. 'The polar bear lifted its great big head and stared straight into my eyes. Luckily I was in Mum's car and she drove off as fast as she could!'

> 'It was seven foot tall and covered in bright white fur.'

Isobel was reading a letter from her pen friend Maggie, a Brownie from Canada. Maggie lived in a small town called Churchill in one of the coldest places on earth. In summer, polar bears visited the town, trudging from their icy homes in the north to scavenge for food.

'Because of global warming, more and more bears come here every year,' read Isobel. 'We have a jail where we put the really naughty ones!' The Brownies laughed.

> 'We have a jail where we put the really naughty ones!'

Since Isobel had been writing to Maggie she had found out lots about polar bears. She knew that during winter huge parts of the sea froze over. The bears would walk on the ice to hunt for food. Everything they ate was stored as fat in their massive bodies so that when the ice melted they had enough food to keep them going throughout the summer.

'What's global warming?' asked Phoebe, a girl from another Six.

Brown Owl explained that fumes from cars and power stations around the world stopped the heat from the sun and the heat created on the earth from escaping back into space. So the earth was gradually getting warmer and warmer and the ice caps were melting.

Isobel chipped in, 'Because of global warming the ice on the sea melts earlier and earlier each year. Now the polar bears can't collect enough food and they might die out.'

The girls felt sad. 'But how can we help the polar bears when they are so far away?' asked one girl.

'But how can we help the polar bears when they are so far away?'

'There', said Brown Owl. The Brownies were puzzled. Brown Owl was pointing at a bin full of drinks cans. 'Those cans can be melted down to make other things – it's called recycling. Do any of your parents recycle their rubbish?' A few hands went up. 'Well that helps to stop the factories making so much pollution. Can you think of other things we do to help the environment?'

'I share a lift to school with my friend – so

that makes less car fumes,' said Phoebe. Isobel told them that she had a light bulb in her bedroom that only used a little bit of electricity. The Brownies were amazed that the things they did at home could affect polar bears on the other side of the world.

'Let's think about other things that we can do to help the environment for our next meeting,' said Brown Owl. Isobel looked out of the window at the Guide hut's garden with its little stream. The garden was full of plastic bags and drinks cans and it wasn't a very nice place for them to play. 'We could clean up out there,' suggested Isobel. 'That's a great idea,' said Brown Owl. The girls agreed and arranged to meet at the hut that Saturday.

On Saturday morning the girls arrived at the Guide hut with their arms full of rubber gloves and bin bags. The air was bitterly cold and it turned the girls' breath to mist. 'It looks like it might snow,' said Brown Owl, looking at the heavy clouds.

'It looks like it might snow'

It was Isobel's job to pick up rubbish from the stream. As she worked she remembered one of Maggie's letters. Her friend lived near the sea and one day she had gone there with her dad. 'The beach is usually clean the letter said, but today there were hundreds of softdrink cans everywhere. They were brought on the tide from countries far away.' Maggie told Isobel that chemicals from factories and farms also travelled across the sea and made the polar bears ill. Isobel looked

'There were hundreds of softdrink cans everywhere'

down at her full bin bag. She was pleased that she was doing something to help.

Just then it started to snow. Great powdery flakes of snow blew in on an icy north wind. The girls ran around and stuck out their tongues to catch the flakes but the wind blew harder and soon they could barely see in front of their faces. 'Let's go inside for a warm drink,' said Brown Owl.

'The wind blew harder and soon they could hardly see in front of their faces'

In the Guide hut, the girls drank hot chocolate and chatted. Outside it snowed… and snowed… and snowed, until the garden, the stream and the town looked like another place, far away on the other side of the world.

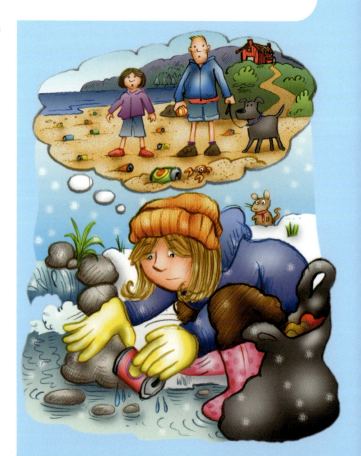

Illustrated by Beccy Blake

The girls talked about all the things they had been doing to help the environment. Some of them had asked their parents about recycling rubbish. Others had started to walk to school and Brownies instead of taking the car.

'Have you thought of any other ideas?' asked Brown Owl. Sarah, a girl from Isobel's Six put up her hand: 'How about turning off our TVs when we've finished watching them?' she said. 'And trying to remember to turn off the taps while we're brushing our teeth. That should save water.' 'Yes' said Brown Owl, 'those are good ideas.' 'And,' said Phoebe, 'we could use both sides of any paper we use.' The Brownies decided to make a checklist of their ideas and tick them off each time they did them.

When it finally stopped snowing the girls went outside. Isobel looked at the town and thought how similar it looked to the photos that she had seen of Maggie's town, Churchill. Perhaps we're not so very far from the polar bears after all, she thought.

> 'Perhaps we're not so very far from the polar bears after all'

When the Brownies' parents began to arrive, the girls had built a giant polar bear out of snow. Isobel remembered that she had forgotten to pick up her rubbish bag and trudged back to get it. Suddenly, something made her jump. Beside the stream there was a huge dent in the snow. She looked closer. Isobel gasped. It was a paw print, very much like a polar bear's…

FAIRY CAKE CREATIONS

Try these recipes using the new Brownie fairy cake mix from Victoria Foods!

CHOCOLATE LOG ROLL

You need

1 Brownie fairy cake mix ★ 1 egg ★ water ★ a 200g bar of fairtrade/organic milk chololate, broken into chunks ★ 100g bar of fairtrade/organic dark chocolate (at least 70% cocoa), broken into chunks ★ 125ml double cream ★ icing sugar ★ non-stick baking parchment

1 Follow the instructions on the packet for mixing the cake mix. Spread the cake mix out evenly into a square baking tin lined with parchment.

Illustrated by Stuart Lynch

2 Place the mix in the oven and bake for 12 minutes. Remove from the oven and allow to cool.

Be safe

3 Make the chocolate log centre. Melt the chocolate with the cream in a heatproof bowl over a saucepan of simmering water. Be careful not to let the bowl touch the water. Add icing sugar to your taste.

4 Spread the melted chocolate evenly over the cake. Roll into a log and set aside while you make the icing from the packet.

5 Spread the icing over the log, decorate with the sugar flowers and share with your friends.

FAIRY CAKE ICE CREAM

You need

1 Brownie fairy cake mix ★ 1 egg ★ water ★ 500ml single cream ★ a tin of condensed milk ★ 2 tsp vanilla extract

BADGE LINK

1 Mix and bake the cake mix as before and set aside. For the ice cream, mix the cream, condensed milk and vanilla extract thoroughly in a bowl until smooth.

2 Cut the cooked fairy cake mix into cubes and mix in with the ice cream mix. Add the sugar flowers if you like.

3 Place the ice cream mix in an empty ice cream container and freeze.

4 Serve the ice cream to your friends the next day!

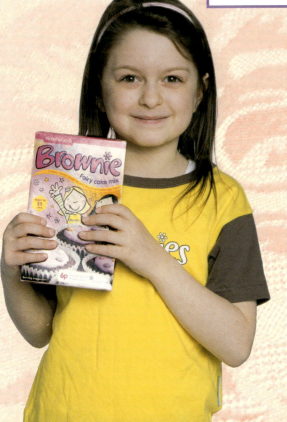

Water world

The oceans cover over two-thirds of our planet. Yet we still know very little about what really goes on deep, deep down below...

Adam Hart-Davis/Science Photo Library

Deep and dark...

Below 1,000 metres the ocean becomes an icy pitch black world. Sunlight cannot reach this far through the water and the only light comes from creatures that glow in the dark, a bit like fireflies. This is called bioluminescence and fish and jellyfish of the deep use it to confuse other creatures that try to eat them.

Aliens down below

Some of the strangest creatures we know live very deep in the oceans. Most have flat bodies and are transparent. Others, like the gulper eel, can swallow prey as big as themselves. The angler fish is covered with antennae and has a flashing light pole on its head. It uses it to attract food to its huge mouth.

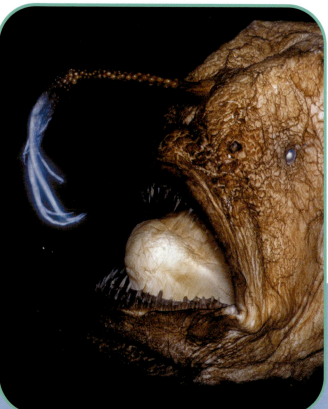

Peter Batson/exploretheabyss.com

How deep?

At 3,000 metres below the surface the ocean floor is the abyssal plain. The abyssal plain covers over half of the earth, but we have explored less than one-hundredth of it. This is because the water pressure this far down would crush a human being like an eggshell. Only five submarines exist that can go this deep.

BADGE LINK

Really, really deep...

In some areas, the ocean floor drops down even deeper than the abyssal plain, into big trenches several thousand metres wide and over 10,000 metres deep. The deepest trench in the world is the Marianas Trench on the Ocean Pacific floor, near the US territory of Guam. It is almost 11,000 metres deep.

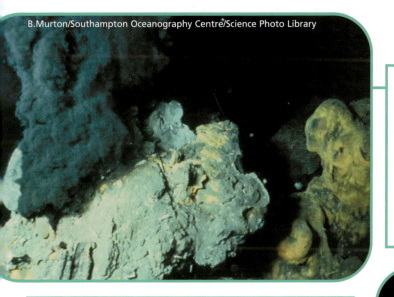

B.Murton/Southampton Oceanography Centre/Science Photo Library

Black smokers

In the deep are creatures that can survive without energy from the sun. Heat from the earth's core pushes minerals up through cracks on the ocean floor, which looks like black smoke. These minerals are why so many creatures, including fish, shellfish and even an octopus, can survive so far down.

Dumbo!

One of the most amazing creatures to be found as far as 7,000 metres down in the ocean is the Dumbo octopus. It is called Dumbo after the cartoon elephant because it has flaps on either side of its head that look like elephant ears. The octopus can flap its 'ears' using them like flippers to swim.

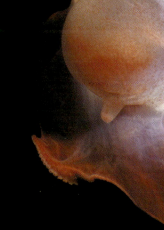

Peter Batson/exploretheabyss.com

More ocean facts

Web safe

❀ On average, a new species in the ocean is discovered every ten days!
❀ Want to find out more about the oceans and creatures down below? Visit www.bbc.co.uk/nature/blueplanet .

WHALE ORIGAMI

Fold your way to the largest mammal on earth – the blue whale!

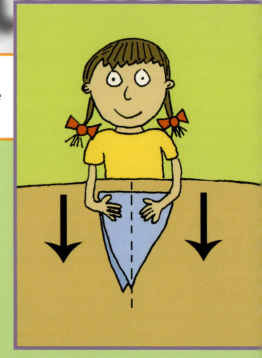

You need
Blue square paper 20x20cm
★ Hole puncher

 1 Crease along the diagonal of the paper then fold the two outside edges into the centre crease.

Fold the other two edges to the centre. **2**

3 Fold in half, with the top point to the bottom point.

 4 Fold in the middle.

Illustrated by Rosie Benham

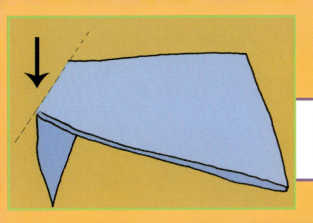

Make a crease where shown then fold the tail inwards to point down.

5

6 Fold one tail point back up so both tail points look equal.

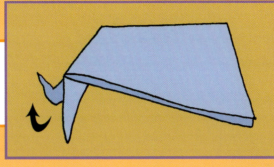

Fold the tips of the tails as shown.

7

Brownies

8 With the hole puncher, create the eyes. Fold the tails to the sides. If you want to, cut a thin strip along the back and fold up to look like a water spout.

9 Make the body as rounded as you can and tuck one side into the other.

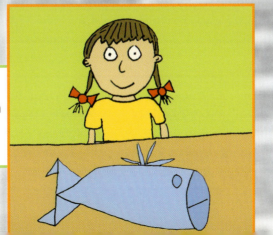

Competition

Show us your cycling knowledge and you could win your very own Brownie bike!

Girlguiding UK in association with Raleigh UK Ltd have produced a special edition Brownie Raleigh bike. The bike features the special Brownie colour and comes with **six-speed gears**. The lucky winner of our competition will receive a free Brownie bike delivered to her address ready to use!

To take part in our competition, show us your knowledge of the highway code rules for cyclists by answering the questions opposite correctly.

The Brownie, as well as Rainbow, bikes are on sale through Girlguiding UK Trading Service, priced at £114.99 (Brownies) and £84.99 (Rainbows). The exclusive bikes are delivered fully constructed, tested and ready for use. A percentage of the sale price goes to Girlguiding UK.

Always stay safe on the road. For cycling safety advice visit **www.cyclesense.net**. To find out about the highway code rules for cyclists visit **www.highwaycode.gov.uk** and follow the link for cyclists.

Web safe

1) What should cyclists wear when out cycling?

2) What should a bicycle have when used at night-time?

3) List three things cyclists are not allowed to do when cycling.

On the back of your entry, write:
- your name
- your age
- your address
- your Brownie Pack
- the three best things in your Brownie Annual
- the best thing about being a Brownie

Send your entry to:
Brownie Annual 2006, Raleigh Bike Competition, Girlguiding UK, 17–19 Buckingham Palace Road, London, SW1W 0PT

The closing date for the competition is 17th February 2006.

Feathered friends

The budgerigar, or budgie, is a friendly bird that loves company and is originally from Australia.

Home sweet home

Domestic budgies are happiest in aviaries with other birds. An aviary is a giant cage kept outside, which can house lots of birds. It should have two sections, a closed one to provide shelter, and an open section in which they can fly around.

Keep it clean

Budgies produce droppings every day and these must be removed daily to prevent the bird getting sick. Once a week give the cage a good clean as well, washing all the cage furniture and perches.

Stephen Dalton/NHPA

Nice and cosy

Budgies can also be kept in a cage. Because they love company it's always better to have more than one budgie. Choose as large a cage as possible with horizontal bars that allows the budgies to climb up and down. Keep the cage in a room where the birds can have lots of human contact and be let out safely every day for excercise.

Yummy tucker

Budgies should be fed mixed seeds shaken in a sieve to get rid of dust. You can find seeds in any pet store. Give occasional treats like fresh lettuce, apple and carrot as well. A cuttlefish bone for them to peck at is also essential.

BADGE LINK

Friend to animals

Watering hole

Budgies need a constant supply of fresh drinking water. They also need fresh water for bathing in a separate container. A shallow dish makes a good bird bath for splashing around in.

Handling and training

Budgies can be trained to land on your finger and can be handled frequently without stress. To pick up a budgie, place one hand over its back. The tail should lie along the inside of your wrist and the head should rest between the first and second fingers, while the thumb and other fingers hold the wings. Be as gentle as possible and never squeeze the bird.

Dave Watts/NHPA

Look who's talking!

Budgies, being little parrots, can be taught to talk. The bird needs to hear a word over and over until it eventually learns to repeat it. It's best to do this training somewhere quiet. You need to be very patient for this as it can take a long time.

It's a budgie life

Web safe

If budgies are loved and well looked after, they can live for up to ten years! To find out more about caring for budgies, look at the official RSPCA pet guide, *Care for your Budgerigar*. You can also visit the RSPCA's website for information at www.rspca.org.uk .

RSPCA

Pet puzzlers

Find your way out of these pet pickles!

Spot ten things wrong with this picture

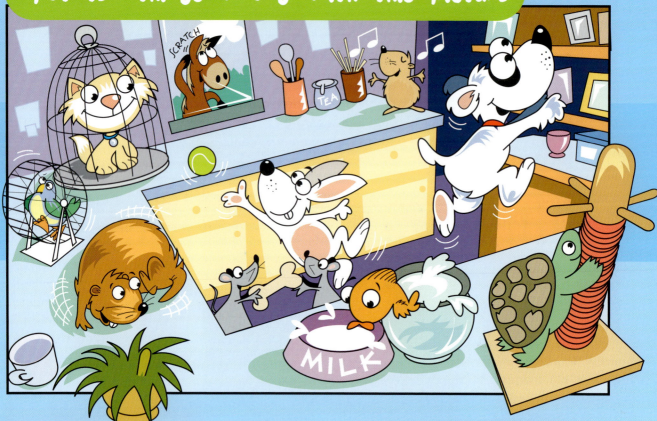

Hamster trail

Which thread should Harvey hamster follow to get to his den?

Find two kittens that match

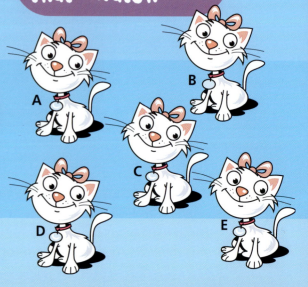

Which lettuce?

Rabbit is very particular about his lettuce and likes them evenly shaped (symmetrical). Which leaf will rabbit eat?

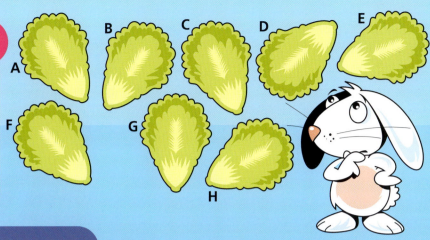

Spot the difference

Illustrated by Nick Diggory

Lead pile-up

In which order should the dog leads be picked up so that the top one is chosen each time?

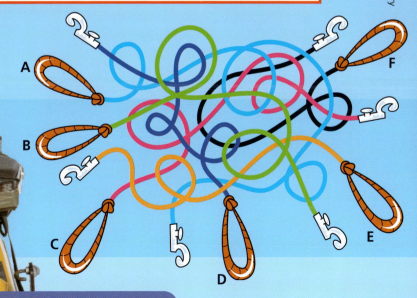

How did you do? Check the answers on page 77!

Why not me?

On the way to Brownies

So what happens at Brownies?

We do lots of activities and have loads of fun.

At the meeting

This is my neighbour Hannah, she wants to find out what Brownies is like.

Welcome Hannah.

This is Hannah, she's visiting Brownies today.

Hello Hannah.

Can I be Hannah's Brownie Buddy today?

Of course you can Kat.

Brownies, we're going to play a game. Can the Sixers come to me please.

What's a Sixer?

Photographs by Laura Ashman

I want to be a Sixer too.

A Sixer's the leader of a Six. Like me, I'm the Sixer for the Squirrels Six.

Everyone, Hannah's decided to join Brownies, so let's give her a big welcome.

As your Brownie Buddy, I'll look after you.

The next week

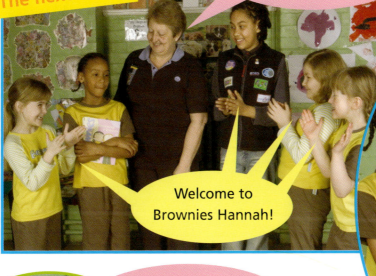

Welcome to Brownies Hannah!

Sarah's leaving us after today, Brownies, because her family's moving away.

I'm going to miss everyone.

Well Fatima's been an excellent Second for Sarah, she'd make a good Sixer.

Here's my chance!

We'll have to pick a new Sixer for the Dolphins Six with Sarah leaving.

Could I be the new Sixer?

Later, on the way home from Brownies

Brownies, we have a new girl today and her name is Amanda.

Hello everyone.

Brown Owl, could I be Amanda's Brownie Buddy please?

Of course you can Hannah.

Hannah's being a really good Brownie Buddy to Amanda.

Hello. I'm Hannah and I'll be your Brownie Buddy.

Thanks Hannah.

Two weeks later

Yes, I was worried Amanda would be very shy but Hannah's really helped her settle in.

I'd like to become a Brownie Buddy too, just like Hannah is to me.

Well that's really nice to hear Amanda.

I still hope to be a Sixer, but I really enjoy looking after my Buddy.

Well you're a really good Buddy, Hannah, and will be an excellent Sixer one day.

Dot to the Rescue

My best friend Genie stayed round at ours one weekend last month. Her parents are both doctors and had to go away for a conference so mum said she could sleep over.

On Sunday morning we wrapped up warm and set off for a long walk in the woods with my dog Wizard – I call him Wizzie for short. Dad kept him on the lead until we reached the stile – that's a funny gate-like thing that you have to climb over at the edge of the woods – and then he was off, chasing about trying to find rabbits (he never does!).

Wizzie had rushed ahead and started barking and scratching at the ground. We thought he'd found a rabbit burrow, but as we got closer we saw he was standing next to a big brown cardboard box.

'Leave it alone Wiz,' said Dad, 'it's just some rubbish someone's left.' But Wizzie wouldn't budge. He just kept barking and whining.

Then we heard a noise – the faintest little meow. Dad lifted the lid – and inside were three tiny kittens, two black and white and one ginger.

'Someone must have dumped them here. Thank goodness we found them,' said Dad. 'Why would anyone do something so mean? They could have died if Wizzie hadn't sniffed them out,' I said.

Dad explained that sadly people often abandoned unwanted animals, especially puppies and kittens, because they couldn't afford to keep them or just simply didn't want them.

'Can we keep them then? They need looking after. We can't just leave them here,' I said.

Dad said there were special places that looked after unwanted animals and found them new homes.

'Remember Dot, we went to the open day at the Cats' Protection League shelter last year and saw all those cats and kittens in their pens? It's a charity that cares for them until a good home can be found. We should take them there,' he said.

We put Wizzie back on his lead and Dad carefully carried the box home and put it on the back seat of his car. Mum brought out a bowl of water because she said the kittens were in danger of being dehydrated (that means they hadn't had a drink for a long while) and we set off for the shelter.

Mum said she'd call to let them know we were on our way and when we arrived a lady called Sue was waiting for us on the drive.

'What have we got here then?' she said.

Dad explained where we'd found the kittens and Sue said they'd be checked over by a vet,

given something to eat and then given a home at the shelter until someone wanted them.

'They'll be microchipped too,' said Sue, 'so that if they ever get lost they can be identified and they'll be neutered so they won't be able to have kittens in the future. People often think it would be lovely to have kittens until they've got them and have to buy food and pay the vet's bills and find homes for them.'

Sue said we could go back and see the kittens whenever we wanted and she promised to let us know if homes were found for them.

When we got home Genie and I went to the Cats' Protection League website to find out more about its work. There are lots of shelters all over the country and nearly all its staff are volunteers. They rely on donations to keep running – and that gave Genie and me an idea.

'Why don't we do something to raise money for them? We could get sponsors and then take all the money up to the shelter to give to Sue,' Genie said.

Mum thought it was a great idea and we decided on a sponsored walk. Dad agreed to do it with us and we took Wizzie along too. We planned a three-mile route from our house and back, and managed to raise £48 between us.

When we went back to the shelter Sue was really pleased with our donation. She asked if we'd like to see the kittens again.

'We've already found homes for them. They'll be leaving this weekend,' she said.

And she had one more surprise for us…

'Do you know what we decided to call them?' she said, 'Dot, Genie and Wizard!'

Find out more about Dot's adventures – visit her at **www.missdorothy.com**.

Web safe

Did you know?

- Cats can be left – or right-pawed, just like humans can be left – or right-handed.
- Cats spend about 16 hours a day sleeping. A 15-year-old cat will have spent ten years of its life asleep.
- A group of kittens is called a kindle and a group of adult cats is a clowder.
- Cats can make more than 100 vocal sounds, dogs can make only about ten.
- Every breed of dog has a pink tongue except the chow, which has a black one.
- Cats rarely meow at each other – the meow is the sound they use for humans.
- The German government came up with the idea for guide dogs for the blind. They trained dogs to help blind war veterans after the First World War.
- Dogs have excellent hearing and can pick up sounds too faint for humans to hear.
- Cats see six times better than humans in the dark.
- A cat has 230 bones in its body – a human has only 206.

HAIR-CLIPPING FUN

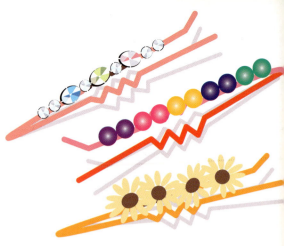

Make the most of your old hair clips for a sparkly new style.

1 Clear a surface on top of a table and put down some old newspaper in case of mess.

2 Paint the surface of each hair clip with a coat of coloured nail varnish. If you like, you could paint one half of the clip in a different colour to the other. Let it dry then apply another coat.

Illustrated by Martina Farrow

3 While the second coat is still wet, carefully but quickly decorate with glitter or beads. You could make a pattern or even write a word, just be sure not to overload the clip. Allow it to dry thoroughly.

BADGE LINK

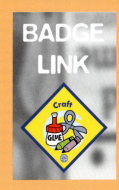

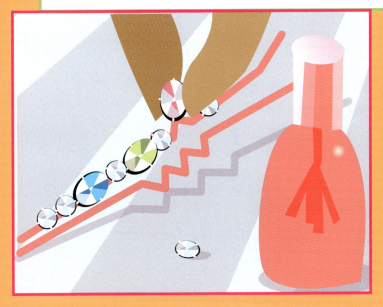

4 Very carefully, paint over the clip with a layer of clear varnish to give a shiny finish and to fix everything in place. Leave to dry again.

5 Clip into your hair for a dazzling new look! If you have enough shades of nail varnish, you could coordinate your hairclips to match your outfits. How about making a special Brownie clip using gold nail varnish?

WINTER OLYMPIC WINNERS!

MEDAL BISCUITS

Show someone in your Pack you think she's number one with these gold medal biscuits!

You need

110g butter, at room temperature, cut into small cubes ★ 50g caster sugar ★ 110g plain flour ★ 50g ground almonds ★ white or yellow icing tubes

1 Preheat your oven to 180°C/Gas Mark 4. Beat the butter and sugar together with an electric whisk or wooden spoon. Gradually add the flour and ground almonds until the mixture forms a thick paste.

Be safe

2 Roll this out on a board that has been lightly dusted with caster sugar until the mixture is about 5mm thick. Using a round cutter, cut out biscuit shapes and place on a lightly greased baking sheet.

3 Bake for 15 mins until golden brown. Carefully lift the biscuits onto a wire rack using a spatula or fish slice and leave to cool completely.

4 Once cold, you can decorate the biscuits with the icing. Why not write what the medal is being awarded for, such as 'Biggest smile' or 'Best listener'?

Brownies

gold smile

silver

Illustrated by Michaela Blunden

SNOWBALL TRUFFLES

These chocolate treats look like the Torino 2006 mascot – Neve the snowball. Don't forget to have a cold drink containing Gliz the ice cube handy!

You need

450g white chocolate, broken into pieces ★ 570ml double cream ★ 50g unsalted butter ★ 25g dessicated coconut ★ mini paper sweet cases

BADGE LINK

1 Melt the chocolate with the cream in a heatproof bowl over a saucepan of simmering water. Be careful not to let the bowl touch the water.

Be safe

2 Once the chocolate has melted, whisk in the butter. Carefully remove the bowl from the pan and continue to whisk until the mixture has thickened. Allow to cool until you can handle it comfortably.

3 Take teaspoons of the chocolate mixture and roll into balls. This can get messy! Roll the balls in the coconut, pressing it in until they are covered.

4 Put the coconut snowballs into paper cases and keep in the fridge until needed. Eat within two days.

It's magic time

Want to dazzle your friends and family? Try with these two simple magic tricks.

Tricky box!

You need
- a coin
- an empty matchbox (ask an adult)

1 Show that the matchbox is empty, then ask a friend to place the coin inside.

2 Close the box and hold it between finger and thumb, with your palm facing you, and give it a shake so the others can hear the coin inside.

3 Now squeeze the sides gently to create a little gap for the coin to drop secretly into your palm.

4 Now take the box with your other hand and put it down on the table, while you secretly slip the coin in your hand into your pocket.

5 Ask someone to open the box and... Hey Presto!

Lucky seven

You need
• a deck of playing cards

1 Prepare your trick first. Find the seven of hearts (or any other suit) and place it face up seventh from the bottom of the deck.

2 To perform the trick, have a friend select a card from the pack. Have the card shown to everyone then place it on top of the deck.

3 Cut the deck in half and place the bottom half over the top half.

4 Tell your audience that you will speak to the cards, and one of them will reveal the chosen card to you.

5 Spread the cards until you come to the upturned seven of hearts and say: "The lucky seven of hearts wants to tell me where the card is."

Photographs by Laura Ashman

6 Starting from the card beneath the seven, count out loud to seven and turn over the seventh card to reveal...

5 A DAY

It's good for you to eat at least five portions of fruit and veg every day. But why? What is a portion? Find out!

Why eat more? (fruit & veg)

🍄 Well, for a start, fruit and vegetables taste great. There are so many to choose from and they come in so many different colours!

🍓 Eating more fruit and vegetables will help fight the two biggest risks to your health when you get older – heart disease and some cancers.

🥔 Fruit and vegetables are full of vitamins and minerals, which we all need to stay healthy and feel great. By staying healthy, you can keep on taking part in all the fun Brownie challenges and other things you enjoy!

What counts?

Fruits and vegetables can also come frozen, canned, dried or as 100% juice and they all count! Of course, nothing is yummier than fresh fruit and veg.

What's a portion?

A portion could be:
★ an apple
★ a cereal bowl of mixed salad
★ two halves of canned peach
★ a pear
★ a banana
★ seven strawberries
★ a tablespoon of raisins
★ two satsumas
★ half a red, yellow or green pepper
★ two plums
★ a glass of pure orange juice
★ three dried apricots
★ three tablespoons of sweetcorn
★ twelve chunks of canned pineapple
★ three tablespoons of cooked kidney beans
★ half a courgette
★ two broccoli florets

Chart it!

To find out if you're getting enough fruit and veg keep a 5-A-DAY diary for two weeks. Draw a 5-A-DAY diagram for one week, like the one below, and make copies. Afterwards, tick each box for every portion you eat everyday. See how you scored for the first week, then see if you can do better the next week. You might do so well you'll need to add extra boxes!

ONE PORTION =

- ☐ 1 medium glass of fruit juice
- ☐ 1 medium-sized fruit
- ☐ 2 spears of broccoli
- ☐ 1 tablespoon of raisins
- ☐ 3 heaped tablespoons of peas

Mark a box with a ✔ or drawing for every portion you eat

5 A DAY   Just Eat More (fruit and veg)

PORTIONS	MON	TUES	WED	THURS	FRI	SAT	SUN
1							
2							
3							
4							
5							
+							

5 A DAY

Logos-a-go-go

Look out for this logo in shops and supermarkets. If you see the logo on a food packet it means that it provides at least one or more portions of fruit and vegetables per serving. Want to find out more about 5 A DAY? Visit **www.5ADAY.nhs.uk** .

Web safe

5-A-DAY DELIGHTS

Now try these super-tasty colourful treats!

BAKED APPLES

You need

4 apples ★ 15g butter ★ 4tbsp blackberries ★ 4tbsp runny honey

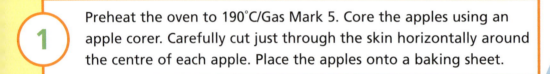

1 Preheat the oven to 190°C/Gas Mark 5. Core the apples using an apple corer. Carefully cut just through the skin horizontally around the centre of each apple. Place the apples onto a baking sheet.

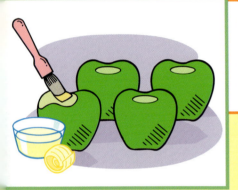

2 Melt the butter and brush it lightly over each apple. Bake for 30-40mins, depending on the size of your fruit.

3 After 20mins, drop the blackberries into the hole in the centre of each apple and return them to the oven for the remaining time.

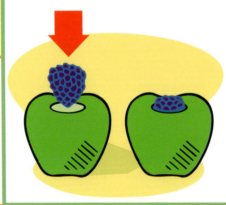

4 Carefully remove the baked apples using a spatula or fish slice and place on a serving plate. Brush them all over with the honey. Serve this scrumptious dessert hot as it is or with a scoop of vanilla ice cream.

Illustrated by John Hallett

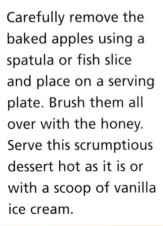

MANGO AND RASPBERRY SMOOTHIE

1 In a blender or food processor, mix the mango, raspberries, banana, yoghurt and milk until smooth. Add a splash more milk if the smoothie seems too thick.

BADGE LINK

You need

1 ripe mango, peeled, stoned and roughly chopped or 1 can mango pieces ★ 225g raspberries ★ 2 bananas, peeled and roughly chopped ★ 400g Greek or natural yoghurt ★ 100ml milk

2 Serve in tall glasses for a brighter breakfast!

OVEN-ROASTED VEGETABLES

You need

4 tbsp olive oil ★ 1 large onion, peeled and chopped ★ 1 aubergine, chopped ★ 1 large courgette, chopped ★ 1 large red or yellow pepper, deseeded and chopped ★ 225g mushrooms, sliced ★ 200g pack cherry tomatoes ★ salt and pepper to season

1 Preheat the oven to 200°C/Gas Mark 6. Mix the onion, aubergine and courgette with the olive oil, salt and pepper and pour onto a large baking sheet, arranging the vegetables into one layer. Roast for 25mins.

2 Mix in the pepper, mushrooms and cherry tomatoes. Put back in the oven for another 20mins.

3 Serve with pasta or as the filling for a delicious and healthy baked potato.

Be safe

Guide to the stars

The BIG GIG – what's it all about? Learn more about the biggest and noisiest event of the year at Guides!

How it all began

The BIG GIG started out in November 2000 as part of a larger event called GIG2K celebrating the new millennium. Over 17,000 Guides, Brownies, Leaders and other guiding members from around the UK gathered at the Millennium Dome in London for the event. Since then, the BIG GIG has become an annual event in its own right open to any member of guiding aged over 10 – including Brownies!

Follow the music

After the Millennium Dome other venues to have staged the BIG GIG include Wembley Arena, the Manchester Evening News Arena (the largest indoor arena in Europe) and the NEC Arena in Birmingham. In 2003 the Wembley Arena concert sold out in just 90 minutes, selling out faster than Justin Timberlake and setting a record!

Let who entertain you?

Acts that have performed at BIG GIG events include some of the most popular artists over the years including Atomic Kitten, Blue, Louise, Geri Haliwell, Busted, Darius, Mis-teeq, Blazin Squad, Big Brovaz, Liberty X, Lemar, Jamelia, Holly Valance, Rachel Stevens and Girls Aloud.

Guides, Guides everywhere…

Selling out year after year, the BIG GIG just keeps getting bigger! By 2005, nearly 100,000 screaming Guides and Leaders (yes, even Leaders can get noisy!) had attended all of the BIG GIGs. The record attendance so far is held by BIG GIG 2004, when 27,000 came to the Manchester Evening News Arena.

What the Guides say

"It's great to get the chance to meet other Guides from across the UK." **Katrina, 6th New Southgate Guides**

"We get pop stars just coming to sing to us Guides which is really cool." **Zoe, 2nd Wymondham Guides**

"The BIG GIG was fab … Please, please, please can you put on another one next year." **10th Durham Guides**

What the stars say

"The atmosphere was really energetic – it was beautiful." **Lemar**

"All BIG GIGs are good because there are only women in the audience." **Liz McClarnon**

"I've met some of the girls and they are really, really cool. They are a brilliant audience." **Rachel Stevens**

"The Scouts don't do anything like this do they? Girls always get one over on the boys!" **Mark Owen**

"With a big gang of girls, you can't go wrong." **Atomic Kitten**

Answers

Spot the difference

In the water

1 and 4 are alike.

What order?

Word maze

How many balls?

There are 41 footballs on the field.

Find the missing piece

Renewable riddles (pages 16–17)

Reduce, reuse or recycle?

Did you spot any of these things?

- running water tap
- empty bottles
- newspapers in the corner
- used batteries next to the torch
- lights on (in daylight)
- old pc in box
- drink and food cans
- plastic bags in drawer
- pair of shoes with one broken heel

How many?

There are 70 wind turbines in total.

Complete the jigsaw

Renewable energy spots

All of the following can be used to provide energy: the sun, wind, water, wood crops, straw crops, animal droppings.

Spot ten differences

Year of the dog puzzlers (pages 36–37)

Animal scramble

If you follow the letter spiral all the way into the middle you should come across all these scrambled words: rat, ox, tiger, rabbit, dragon, snake, horse, sheep, monkey, rooster, dog & pig.

Buddha's maze

The snake will get there first.

Missing piece

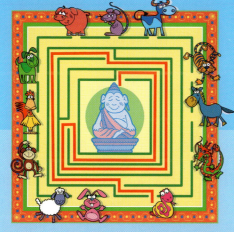

Word maze

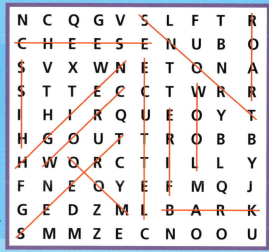

Monkey tricks A

Pet puzzlers (pages 56–57)

Spot ten things wrong

1. Cat in birdcage.
2. Budgie running in hamster wheel.
3. Rabbit playing catch.
4. Hamster chasing its tail.
5. Goldfish drinking out of milk bowl.
6. Pony seen through window scratching ear.
7. Tortoise scratching scratchpost.
8. Mice with a dogbone.
9. Dog climbing up book shelf.
10. Guinea pig singing.

Hamster trail B

Find two kittens that match C & D

Which lettuce? A

Spot the difference

Lead pile-up

In order, B, E, D, C and F.

G'day mate!

Yikes! Saltwater crocs ahead! Go back 1.

21

DARW[IN]

20

19

You catch a boat to Darwin! Go to 21.

13

18

Get a ride with some emus! Go on 1.

Sheep everywhere! No way through! Go back 1.

12   14   17

11   15   16

Oops! Trip over a wombat hole. Go back 1.

10

9   8

Stop to admire a baobab tree. Miss a go.

7

Hitch a ride with some red kangaroos! Go on 3.

6

5

You've arrived in Perth, Australia, to watch the Commonwealth Game[s] but they're in Melbourne! See the sights down under and still get to the Games on time!

OH NO! Bogged down in sand. Go back 1.

4

3

PERTH

2

1

START

You need

a die ★ counters

How to play

Throw the die and follow the instructions to move around the board. First to finish wins.

Off to a flyer! Go on 1.

Illustrated by Andi Good